Mysterious Nature

SINGING SAND DUNES

BY LISA OWINGS

BELLWETHER MEDIA • MINNEAPOLIS, MN

Torque brims with excitement perfect for thrill-seekers of all kinds. Discover daring survival skills, explore uncharted worlds, and marvel at mighty engines and extreme sports. In *Torque* books, anything can happen. Are you ready?

This edition first published in 2025 by Bellwether Media, Inc.

No part of this publication may be reproduced in whole or in part without written permission of the publisher. For information regarding permission, write to Bellwether Media, Inc., Attention: Permissions Department, 6012 Blue Circle Drive, Minnetonka, MN 55343.

Library of Congress Cataloging-in-Publication Data

LC record for Singing Sand Dunes available at: https://lccn.loc.gov/2024009423

Text copyright © 2025 by Bellwether Media, Inc. TORQUE and associated logos are trademarks and/or registered trademarks of Bellwether Media, Inc. Bellwether Media is a division of Chrysalis Education Group.

Editor: Rebecca Sabelko   Designer: Josh Brink

Printed in the United States of America, North Mankato, MN.

TABLE OF CONTENTS

SONG OF THE DESERT	4
WHAT ARE SINGING SAND DUNES?	6
SAND SPIRITS	10
COMING TO THE SURFACE	16
GLOSSARY	22
TO LEARN MORE	23
INDEX	24

Song of the Desert

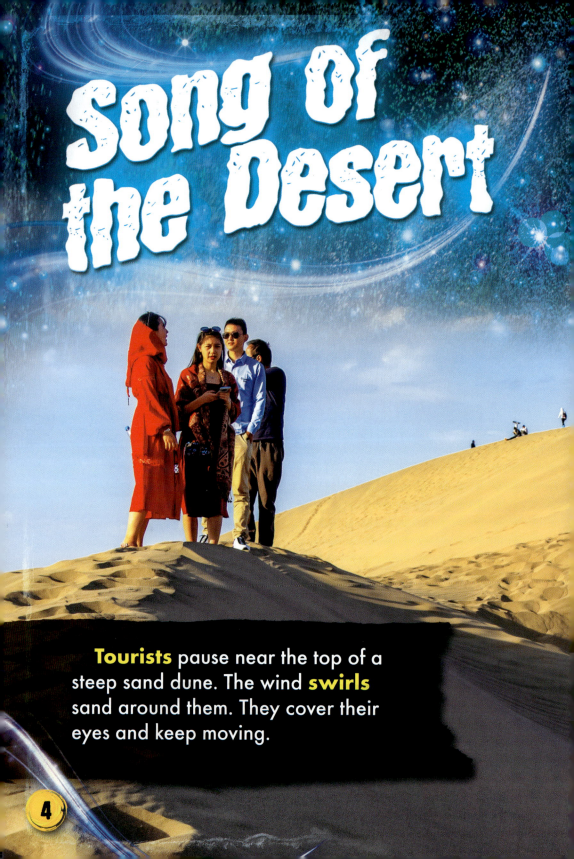

Tourists pause near the top of a steep sand dune. The wind **swirls** sand around them. They cover their eyes and keep moving.

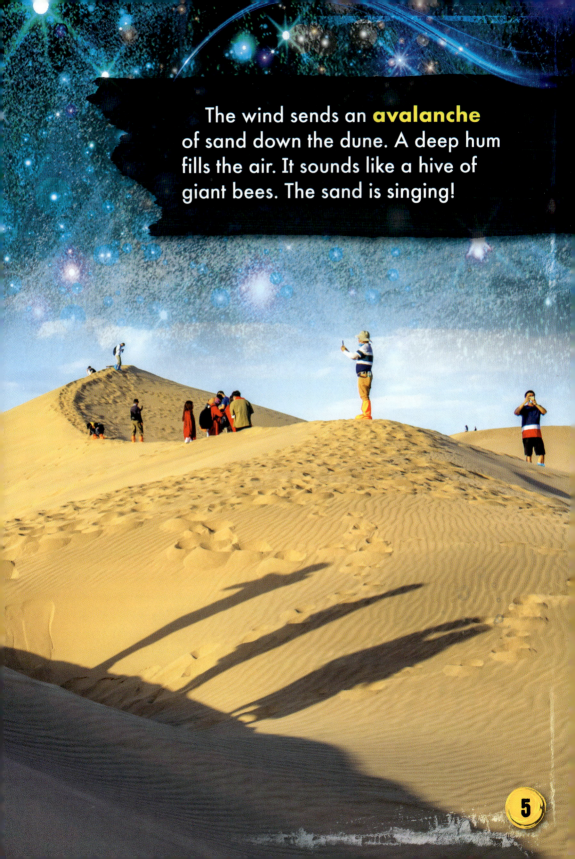

The wind sends an **avalanche** of sand down the dune. A deep hum fills the air. It sounds like a hive of giant bees. The sand is singing!

What Are Singing Sand Dunes?

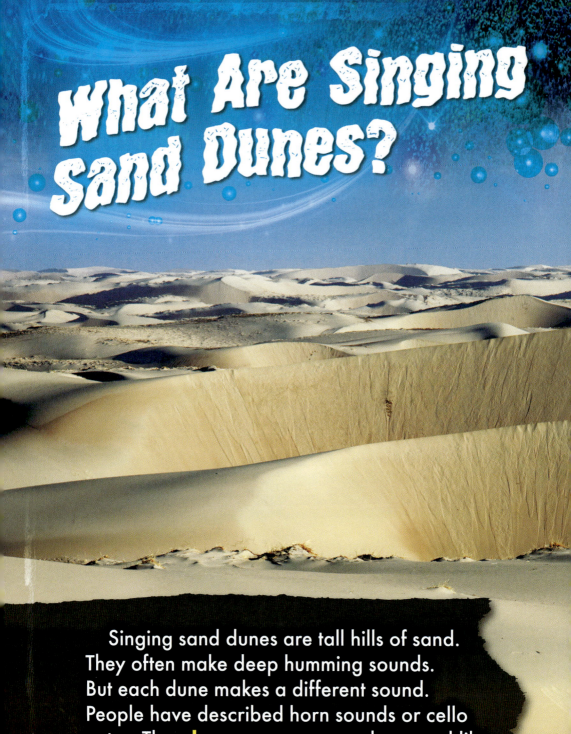

Singing sand dunes are tall hills of sand. They often make deep humming sounds. But each dune makes a different sound. People have described horn sounds or cello notes. The **phenomenon** can also sound like someone burping or an airplane flying.

LONG AND LOUD

Some large dunes can sing for up to 15 minutes. The loudest ones can be heard more than 6 miles (10 kilometers) away.

A dune's song can last for several minutes. The sound can become very loud. The **vibration** it creates can knock people off their feet.

Singing sand dunes are rare. There are about 30 singing sand dunes in deserts and on beaches around the world.

Squeaky Beaches

♪ Noisy sand can also be found on beaches. Each footstep causes sand to make a short squeak. Sand grains must be smooth and round to squeak.

Conditions must be just right for dunes to sing. The best time to hear singing sand dunes is on very dry, windy days. Thin layers of sand can often be seen flowing down the dunes.

Sand Spirits

People crossing deserts have heard singing dunes since long ago. Many believed the sound came from spirits, gods, or **demons**.

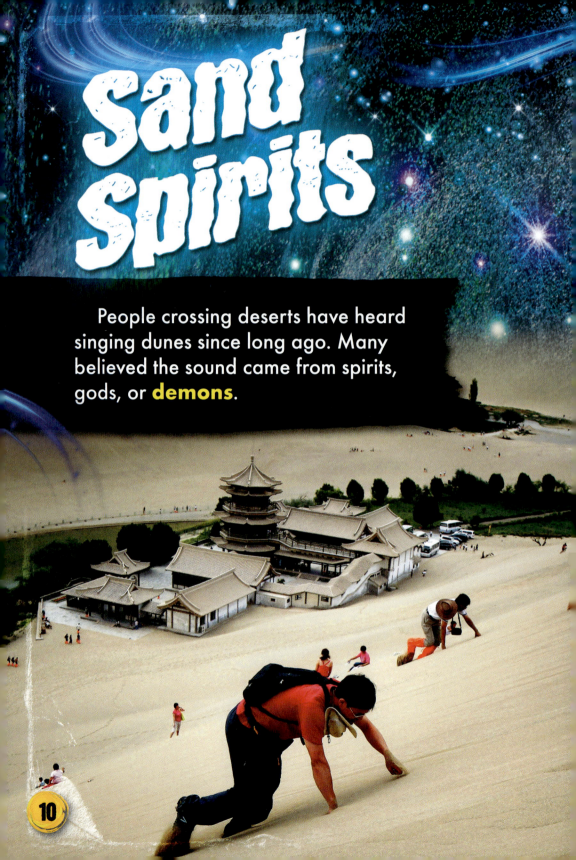

The Snake of Sand Mountain

 Who believes it? Paiute-Shoshone people

 Where? Sand Mountain, Nevada

 What do they believe? The singing on Sand Mountain is the hissing of Kwansee, an ancient snake who moved into the mountain after his wife died. It is believed his hisses are the sounds of him crying out for his wife.

In the 800s CE, a singing dune in China was a **divine** sight. People climbed the dune on a special holiday to hear its song. Today, people make the dune sing during the Dragon Boat Festival.

Marco Polo wrote of singing dunes in the 1200s. He believed evil spirits were speaking to him as he crossed the Gobi Desert in China. He wrote that he heard the sounds of drums and other instruments.

Charles Darwin noted strange sounds in the 1800s. Locals in Chile told him of a hill that roared and **bellowed**.

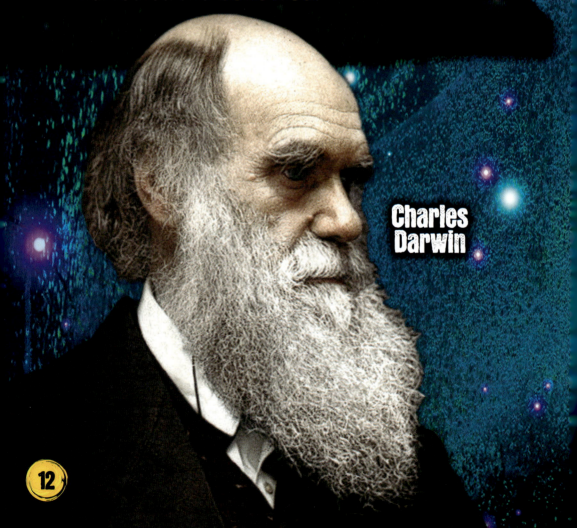

Charles Darwin

Marco Polo

Megadunes

- **Who explored them?** Marco Polo
- **Where?** Gobi Desert
- **When?** 1295
- **What did they believe?** Marco Polo wrote about the giant Badain Jaran dunes. He said they sounded like voices or drums. He also heard sounds like metal clashing or many instruments playing.

In the 2000s, scientists recorded **sound waves** and vibrations from singing sand dunes. They also noted what the weather was like when dunes sang.

Scientists wondered if the sound came from deep within dunes or from grains of sand. They discovered sounds came from the movements of grains of sand!

BACK AT THE LAB

In 2012, researchers took more than 300 pounds (136 kilograms) of sand from singing dunes. They brought it to their lab in Paris. They made mini avalanches. They recreated the sounds!

Coming to the Surface

Scientists still have questions about how singing dunes work. They know the songs happen at the surface of dunes.

SAND NOTES

Each singing dune makes a different note. The note depends on the size of the sand grains.

The grains of sand on singing dunes share special **traits**. They are dry, smooth, and round. Sand grains near each other tend to be about the same size.

Avalanches push a thin layer of surface sand down a big, steep dune. The sand grains slide over the still sand beneath them.

How Dunes Sing

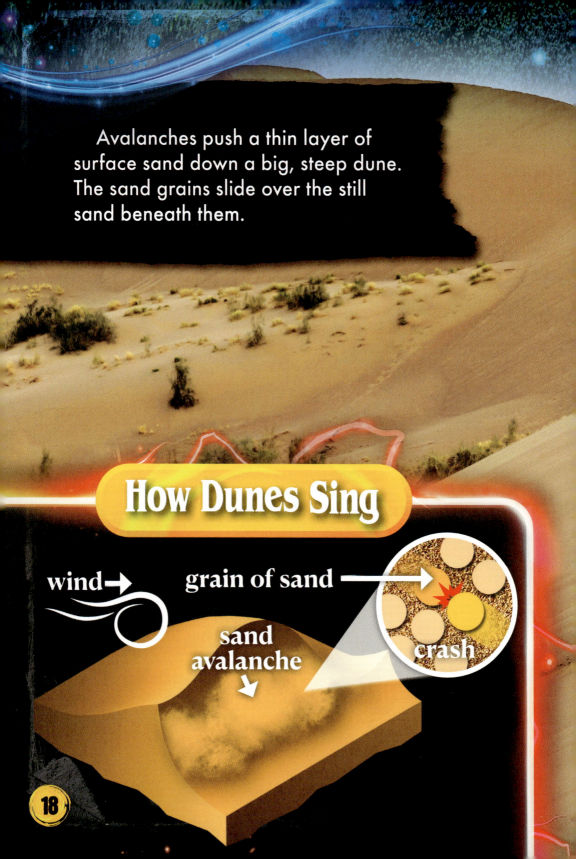

wind →
grain of sand → crash
sand avalanche

SINGING SLIDE

Scientists cannot always wait for winds to cause avalanches. They have to create them. They slide down dunes on their bottoms. They push the sand as they go!

The grains of sand bump into each other as they spill down the dune. Scientists think all these tiny crashes add up to one big sound.

Scientists have another idea about how dunes sing. Sound waves from a dune's surface may bounce off **damp** sand deeper down. This could **amplify** the sound by pushing sound waves into the air.

Scientists will keep studying singing sand dunes. Their desert songs still have an air of mystery.

GLOSSARY

amplify—to make louder or greater

avalanche—a large amount of snow, ice, sand, or earth that suddenly slides down a steep slope

bellowed—made a loud, deep sound

damp—slightly wet

demons—evil spirits

divine—related to a god

phenomenon—an event or fact that can be seen or felt

sound waves—the movements of sound

swirls—moves in a twisting, circular pattern

tourists—people who travel to visit another place

traits—qualities that make one thing different from another

vibration—movement caused by something moving quickly back and forth

TO LEARN MORE

AT THE LIBRARY

Dahl, Michael. *Sound Waves.* North Mankato, Minn.: Capstone Press, 2021.

Maloney, Brenna. *Desert.* New York, N.Y.: Children's Press, 2024.

Nargi, Lela. *Desert Biomes.* Minneapolis, Minn.: Jump!, 2023.

ON THE WEB

FACTSURFER

Factsurfer.com gives you a safe, fun way to find more information.

1. Go to www.factsurfer.com

2. Enter "singing sand dunes" into the search box and click 🔍.

3. Select your book cover to see a list of related content.

INDEX

avalanche, 5, 15, 18, 19
beaches, 8, 9
Chile, 12
China, 11, 12
conditions, 9
Darwin, Charles, 12
demons, 10
deserts, 8, 10, 12, 21
Dragon Boat Festival, 11
explanation, 14, 16, 17, 18, 19, 20
Gobi Desert, 12
gods, 10
history, 10, 11, 12, 13, 14, 15
how dunes sing, 18

megadunes, 13
Polo, Marco, 12, 13
sand, 4, 5, 6, 9, 14, 15, 16, 17, 18, 19, 20
Sand Mountain, 11
song, 7, 11, 16, 21
sound waves, 14, 20
sounds, 5, 6, 7, 10, 12, 14, 15, 19, 20
spirits, 10, 12
squeaky beaches, 9
tourists, 4
vibration, 7, 14
wind, 4, 5, 9, 19

The images in this book are reproduced through the courtesy of: S Terekhov, front cover (hero), back cover; Dan-Rus, pp. 2-3, 8-9, 14-15, 22-24; NGCHIYUI, pp. 4-5; Vladimir Kondrachov/ Alamy, pp. 6-7; ColsTravel/ Alamy, p. 9; Feng Li/Staff/ Getty Images, pp. 10-11; AJ9, p. 11; John G. Murdoch/ Wiki Commons, p. 12 (Charles Darwin); Salviati/ Wiki Commons, p. 13 (Marco Polo); Pascal Goetgheluck/ ScienceSourceImages, p. 15; Sergey Dzyuba/ Alamy, pp. 16-17; Alexey Belonogov, p. 18 (how dunes sing); Terry Allen/ Alamy, pp. 18-19; Marina Pissarova/ Alamy, pp. 20-21.